D1119919

PAKISTAN

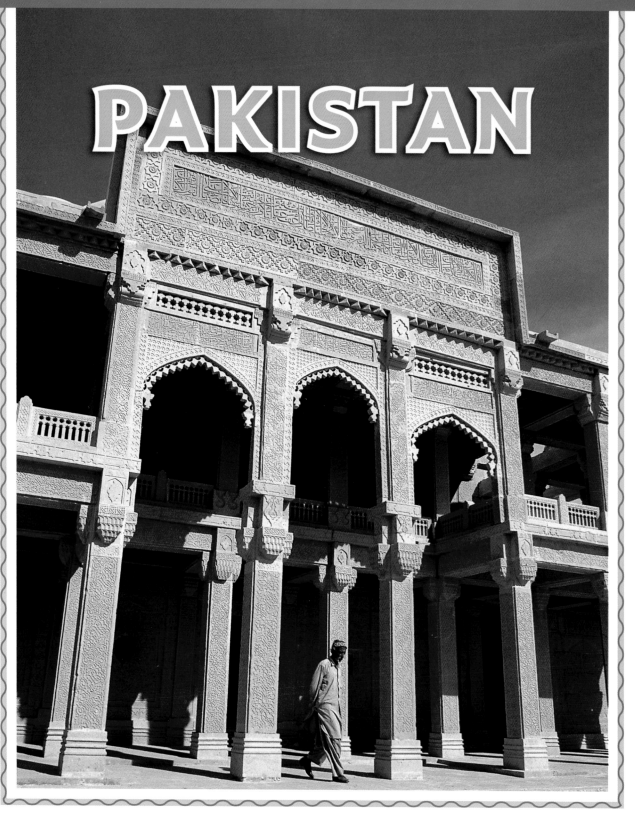

 **Marshall Cavendish** Benchmark

New York

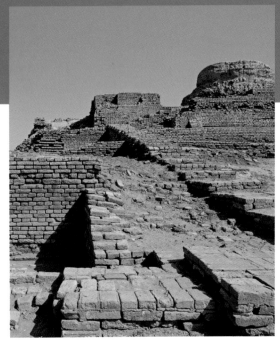

Written by: Karen Kwek and Jameel Haque
Editor: Peter Mavrikis, Cheryl Sim
Publisher: Michelle Bisson
Series Designer: Benson Tan

Photo research by Thomas Khoo

Originated and designed by Marshall Cavendish International (Asia) Pte Ltd
Copyright © 2011 Marshall Cavendish International (Asia) Pte Ltd
Published by Marshall Cavendish Benchmark
An imprint of Marshall Cavendish Corporation
All rights reserved.

This publication represents the opinions and views of the authors based on
Karen Kwek and Jameel Haques' personal experience, knowledge, and research.
The information in this book serves as a general guide only. The authors and
publisher have used their best efforts in preparing this book and disclaim liability
rising directly and indirectly from the use and application of this book.

Other Marshall Cavendish Offices:
Marshall Cavendish International (Asia) Pte Ltd, 1 New Industrial Road,
Singapore 536196 • Marshall Cavendish International (Thailand) Co Ltd.
253 Asoke, 12th Flr, Sukhumvit 21 Road, Klongtoey Nua, Wattana,
Bangkok 10110, Thailand • Marshall Cavendish (Malaysia) Sdn Bhd,
Times Subang, Lot 46, Subang Hi-Tech Industrial Park, Batu Tiga,
40000 Shah Alam, Selangor Darul Ehsan, Malaysia

Marshall Cavendish is a trademark of Times Publishing Limited.
All websites were available and accurate when this book was sent to press.

Library of Congress Cataloging-in-Publication Data
Kwek, Karen.
Pakistan / written by Karen Kwek and Jameel Haque.
p. cm. — (Welcome to my country)
Includes bibliographical references and index.
Summary: "An overview of the history, geography, government, economy,
language, people, and culture of Pakistan. Includes numerous color photos,
a detailed map, useful facts, and detailed resource section"
—Provided by publisher.
ISBN 978-1-60870-158-2
1. Pakistan—Juvenile literature. I. Haque, Jameel. II. Title.
DS376.9.K94 2011
954.91—dc22   2010000355

Printed in Malaysia
135642

PHOTO CREDITS
Alamy: 2, 10, 24
Art Directors & TRIP Photo Library: 6, 11, 27, 28, 32, 34 (bottom),
   35, 43
Corbis: cover
Getty Images: 12, 16, 17, 19, 36
Getty Images/Hulton Archive: 13, 14, 16, 39
Hutchison Library: 3 (center), 5, 20
John R. Jones: 45
Lonely Planet Images: 8, 26
Nik Wheeler: 1, 3 (bottom), 4, 22, 31 (top), 33
Pakistan High Commission, Singapore: 15 (top)
Pakistan National Council of the Arts: 30 (both), 31 (bottom)
Photolibrary: 34 (top), 38
Topham Picturepoint: 3 (top), 7, 9 (both), 15 (center), 15 (bottom), 18,
   21, 23, 25, 29, 37, 40, 41

Contents

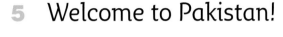

Words that appear in the glossary are printed in **boldface** type the first time they occur in the text.

Markets on the streets of Pakistan's big cities sell food and craft items. This market is in Peshawar.

Welcome to Pakistan!

Pakistan is a young country in South Asia. It was once part of India, ruled by the British, but in 1947 it became a separate nation. The country's official name is Islamic Republic of Pakistan. Although its population includes many **ethnic** groups, almost all of the people are Muslims. Let's explore beautiful Pakistan and meet its **diverse** people.

The Prime Minister's Secretariat Building is a magnificent government office structure in the city of Islamabad, the capital of Pakistan.

The Flag of Pakistan

Pakistan's flag is green with a vertical white stripe down the left side. Green stands for the country's Muslim majority. White represents people of other faiths. The **crescent** and five-pointed star are traditional symbols of the Islamic religion.

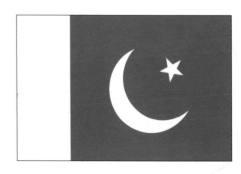

The Land

Pakistan's southern boundary is on the Arabian Sea. Moving clockwise from the southwest to the southeast, Pakistan is surrounded by the countries of Iran, Afghanistan, China, and India.

In an area of 310,402 square miles (803,940 square kilometers), Pakistan has mountain ranges, flatlands, and deserts. K2, in the Karakoram mountain range, is the country's highest point. K2 rises 28,252 feet (8,611 meters).

Stretching across northern Pakistan, the Karakoram Mountains form one of the world's highest mountain ranges. In fact, K2, Pakistan's highest peak, is also the world's second-highest mountain.

Many rivers in Pakistan, including the Indus River, start in the mountainous Hindu Kush, along the country's northwestern boundary. The Himalayas also stretch across northern Pakistan.

In central and southeastern Pakistan, the Indus River, which is the country's main waterway, crosses an area of flat, **fertile** land known as the Indus Plain. This plain is an important agricultural area, especially in the northeastern province of Punjab.

At the southern end of the plain, the province of Sindh has fertile land along the Indus River, but the rest of the land is very dry. The rugged landscape of the southwestern Balochistan **Plateau** is also very dry. Few people live there.

Climate

In northern Pakistan, summers are mild, but winters are cold, with temperatures often below freezing. Southern areas are warmer. In the Indus Plain, summer temperatures range from 90° to 120° Fahrenheit (32° to 49° Celsius), falling to only about 55° F (13° C) during the winter.

Areas along the Arabian Sea have a **humid** climate. Otherwise, Pakistan is very dry and gets little rainfall. The northern areas get the most rain.

During spring in northwestern Pakistan, the mountaintops are still covered with snow when the apricot trees start to bloom.

The Siberian ibex is a type of wild goat with huge horns. It lives in the mountains of northern Pakistan.

Plants and Animals

A variety of trees grow in Pakistan. Areas close to the sea have mangrove forests. The drier southern regions have mulberry trees and date palms. Oak, spruce, and pine trees grow in northern forests. Only small **alpine** plants survive high in the mountains.

The mountains are also home to bears and leopards, while jackals, wild cats, and foxes are found throughout the country. Pakistan's birds include eagles, falcons, wood ducks, and geese.

The snow leopard is an endangered animal that lives in the mountains of northern Pakistan. This shy, majestic animal is not often seen because its fur blends in with its surroundings.

History

People have been living in what is now Pakistan for over eight thousand years. The Indus Valley **civilization**, which is considered one of the world's first great civilizations, lived there over four thousand years ago and **flourished** for about a thousand years. Then, **Aryans** moved in from Central Asia, bringing a form of the Hindu religion with them. Between 500 BCE and 700 CE, many empires and kingdoms ruled the area.

The ancient city of Mohenjo-Daro was one of many well-planned cities built by the Indus Valley civilization.

This painting shows the Mughal emperor Akbar the Great passing the crown to his son, Prince Salim, who was later known as Jahangir.

Islam and the Mughal Empire

Arab Muslims brought Islam to Sindh in the seventh and eighth centuries. From 1206 until the end of the Mughal Empire, Muslim rulers controlled most of India, including the land that is now Pakistan. The Mughal Empire was one of the most famous of India's Muslim kingdoms. From 1526 until the early eighteenth century, its strong leaders continually expanded Mughal territory. Mughal rulers promoted literature, art, architecture, and music and, although Muslim, encouraged religious freedom.

In 1947, Muslim leader Muhammad Ali Jinnah (**extreme right**) met with British and Hindu leaders to discuss dividing British India by religions. When the Hindus and Muslims could not agree on the division, the Indian Independence Act of 1947 created a separate Muslim nation called Pakistan.

British Rule

As the Mughal Empire weakened, the British, who had been trading in India since the 1600s, gained power. In 1858, they took over many Indian territories, which became known as British India.

Britain made many improvements to British India, including introducing the British education system. By the early 1900s, however, Indians wanted a stronger voice in government, and Muslims wanted a separate country.

Independence

On August 14, 1947, Pakistan became an independent country divided into East Pakistan and West Pakistan. As the new nation struggled with unstable leadership and a poor economy, East Pakistan became increasingly unhappy with West Pakistan and wanted more power in government. In 1971, fighting broke out between East and West Pakistan. Millions of civilians from East Pakistan fled to India for **refuge**. India showed its support for East Pakistan's struggle for independence by taking over the country and entering the war against West Pakistan. When India won the war, East Pakistan became a separate country called Bangladesh, while West Pakistan simply became known as Pakistan.

By 1971, the unrest between East and West Pakistan had started a civil war. **Sikh** soldiers from East Pakistan fought for freedom from West Pakistan. On December 16, 1971, East Pakistan became Bangladesh.

A Troubled Country

The breakup of Pakistan did not bring peace. In 1977, Zulfikar Ali Bhutto, who had been the president of West Pakistan, was forced out of office by army general Muhammad Zia ul-Haq. After Zia died in 1988, Zulfikar's daughter, Benazir Bhutto, became prime minister. When she was forced out in 1990, Nawaz Sharif was elected prime minister. Bhutto regained control in 1993. Sharif was reelected in 1996. In October 1999, Pakistan's leadership changed again, following a **coup** led by General Pervez Musharraf. In September 2008, Asif Ali Zardari was elected as the current president of Pakistan.

A soldier standing guard outside the Punjab Assembly offices in Lahore.

Benazir Bhutto (1953—2007)

Named Pakistan's prime minister in 1988, Benazir Bhutto became the first woman to lead an Islamic country. In 1990, she was accused of **corruption** and was forced out of power. She returned to office in 1993 but was forced out again in 1996. Her return to politics was cut short after she was killed in a bomb attack in 2007.

Benazir Bhutto

Liaquat Ali Khan (1895—1951)

In 1923, Liaquat Ali Khan joined Muhammad Ali Jinnah in the fight for Pakistan's independence. In 1947, he became the new nation's first prime minister.

Liaquat Ali Khan

Imran Ahmed Khan Niazi (1952—)

Considered one of Pakistan's best cricket players, Imran Ahmed Khan Niazi led the country's national team to victory in the 1991–1992 World Cup competition. He retired from cricket in 1992 and entered politics.

Imran Ahmed Khan Niazi

The Government and the Economy

Pakistan is a **federal republic** led by a president and a prime minister. The president is the head of state and the prime minister is the head of government. A **parliament** elects both government leaders and makes the country's laws.

During Musharraf's reign as president, he formed the National Security Council, which is now Pakistan's most powerful governing body.

President of Pakistan Asif Ali Zardari speaks at the United Nations' sixty-fourth General Assembly at the UN headquarters. Beside him is a photograph of his wife, the late Benazir Bhutto, who was a former prime minister of Pakistan.

This building in Islamabad is the home of the Supreme Court, which is Pakistan's highest court. Another federal court, called the Shari'a Court, tries cases according to Islamic law. Provinces have high courts, as well as district and village courts.

Provinces and Local Governments

Pakistan is made up of four provinces: Balochistan, Sindh, Punjab, and North-West Frontier. Each of these provinces is run by a governor, who reports to a chief minister. The government of each province is broken down into divisions, and each division into districts.

Besides its four provinces, Pakistan also has eleven Federally Administered Tribal Areas and the Islamabad Capital Territory. The local governments for these areas report directly to Pakistan's current president, Asif Ali Zardari.

The Arabian Sea, off Pakistan's southern coast, provides a variety of fish, including salmon, mackerel, and shrimp. These fishermen are unloading a day's catch at Karachi's fishing harbor.

A Struggling Economy

Since becoming an independent nation, Pakistan has struggled to improve its economy. Problems such as an unstable government, a fast-growing population, and increasing debt to other countries have made Pakistan poor.

Almost half of Pakistan's workforce is involved in agriculture. Most of the country's farms are in Punjab, which has flat land and a good water supply.

Industry and Resources

Less than 20 percent of Pakistan's workforce have manufacturing jobs. The most important manufacturing industry is cotton fabrics, or textiles. Other industries produce paper, food products, and construction materials.

Coal mining is one of Pakistan's oldest industries, but the quality of the coal is very poor. The country's other natural resources include petroleum, natural gas, copper, and iron ore.

Because most of Pakistan's farms do not have modern machinery, workers must use traditional farming methods.

People and Lifestyle

The people of Pakistan belong to many ethnic groups. Each group has its own culture, language, and traditions. The five main groups are Punjabis, Sindhis, Pashtuns, Baloch, and Muhajirs (moo-HAH-jeerz).

Pakistan's largest ethnic group, the Punjabis, make up about two-thirds of the population. Because Punjabis live in the fertile Punjab province, most of them have agricultural jobs.

These girls are from an Islamic school in Sindh province. Over the centuries, people from many different cultures settled in this area. Most Sindhis are actually a mixture of ethnic groups, including Persian, Turkish, and Arab.

These elderly men are spending some leisure time in the breathtaking countryside of northern Punjab province. Elderly people in Pakistan are usually treated with great respect.

Most Pashtuns live in North-West Frontier province, but some live in the northern part of Balochistan province. Their **ancestors** were ancient Aryans.

The ancestors of the Baloch people are from Syria. They came to the area that is now Balochistan over fourteen centuries ago. The Baloch lifestyle is growing crops and raising animals.

Muhajirs are Muslims from India. They settled in Pakistan around the time it became a separate nation. Most Muhajirs live in Pakistan's large cities.

Family Life

Pakistani families are often large, and many generations of relatives may live together in the same household. The oldest male family member is the head of the household. Traditionally, men work to support the family, while women run the household and raise the children.

Members of Pakistani families depend on each other and spend a lot of time together. This large family in the city of Lahore is taking a ride together in a horse-drawn carriage.

This mother and her children live in North-West Frontier province. Like so many of Pakistan's people, they face health problems because of poor sewage disposal and a shortage of safe drinking water.

City and Countryside

In the cities of Pakistan, rich people live in large, modern houses, but most city dwellers live in small, old houses in crowded neighborhoods. Large cities are so crowded that almost one-fourth of the people live in **shantytowns**.

Houses in countryside villages are usually made of mud bricks and straw. Some houses in the villages do not even have electricity or running water. The living conditions in many parts of Pakistan are poor and can lead to serious health risks.

Education

The education system in Pakistan has five levels. Elementary school is for children between the ages of five and ten. Middle school, for children aged ten to thirteen, is followed by two years of high school. After high school, some students attend an intermediate college, or higher secondary school, for two more years. To attend a university, a student must pass an examination at the end of the second year of intermediate college.

Both boys and girls attend this elementary school, but in most parts of the country, boys and girls attend separate schools. Traditionally, in Pakistan, educating boys is considered more important than educating girls.

Many rural schools do not have enough classrooms. This schoolteacher from Balochistan province is giving a lesson to some elementary school children outdoors.

Literacy and Other Problems

Less than half of the Pakistani people over the age of fifteen can read and write. The **literacy** rate is lower among the people who live in the countryside because they have fewer opportunities for education. Pakistan does not have enough schools, especially in rural areas, and these schools usually do not have enough trained teachers and classroom materials.

Religion

Islam is Pakistan's official religion. About 97 percent of the country's population are Muslims from one of two main groups. Sunni Muslims are the largest Islamic group. About 75 percent of the country's Muslims are Sunni. The other main group is Shi'ite Muslims. Only about 3 percent of the people in Pakistan are not Muslims. Most of them are Hindus or Christians. Others are Sikhs, Parsis, or Buddhists.

Badshahi Mosque is one of the places Muslims in Lahore go to pray. This huge, red sandstone structure was built in the late 1600s by Mughal emperor Aurangzeb.

The city of Lahore has a small number of people who belong to the Sikh religion. This building is a Sikh temple, which is called a *gurdwara*.

The Islamic Faith

All Muslims believe in one God, called Allah, and His prophet, or messenger, named Muhammad. In practicing their faith, Muslims pray to Allah five times a day. They are also expected to give money to the poor. Each year during the holy month of Ramadan, Muslims do not eat or drink anything during the day. Every Muslim also tries to visit the holy city of Mecca at least once in his or her lifetime.

Language

With so many ethnic groups, Pakistan also has many languages, but only two, Urdu and English, are the country's official languages. Urdu is much like Hindi, the language of India, except it uses many Persian and Arabic words, and it is written from right to left. Though many Pakistanis are unable to speak English, it is still widely used in government, business, and higher education.

Most of the newspapers and magazines that are published in Pakistan are written in Urdu, English, or one of a few other languages. Many Pakistanis speak their own ethnic languages, which include Balochi, Brahui, Punjabi, Pashtu, and Sindhi.

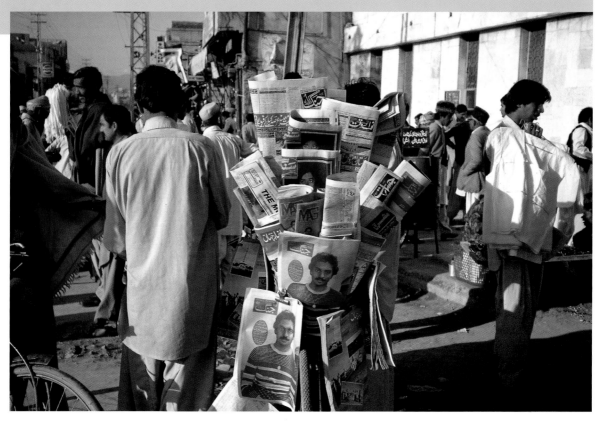

These Muslim boys attend a religious school in Karachi. They are reading the Koran, which is the holy book of the Islamic faith.

Literature

Since the sixteenth century, most of Pakistan's literature has been written in Urdu. Faiz Ahmad Faiz (1911–1984) was a well-known Urdu poet, while Saadat Hasan Manto (1912–1955) is remembered for his short stories. Ahmad Nadeem Qasimi (1916–2006) wrote about life in the countryside. Muhammad Iqbal (1877–1938) is considered Pakistan's most famous poet. Although he died before Pakistan became a nation, he was the first to propose forming an independent state for Muslims.

Arts

During the time of the Mughal Empire, painting was an important art form. The styles developed by Mughal painters are still reflected in Pakistani art today. The works of Pakistan's leading painter, Abdur Rahman Chughtai (1897–1975), are done in traditional Mughal style.

Modern art came to Pakistan in the 1950s. Pakistani artists of the twentieth century, such as Shakir Ali (1916–1975) and Zubeida Agha (1922–1997), used Western painting techniques.

Sadequain (1930–1987) was one of Pakistan's leading modern artists. These pictures show two of his figure paintings. His other works included **murals** and calligraphy.

Art on Wheels

Trucks and buses painted with brightly colored designs are popular throughout Pakistan. The designs can be anything from flowers and landscapes to animals and airplanes. The designs on some vehicles include verses from the Koran.

Decorated trucks like this one are a modern art form in Pakistan.

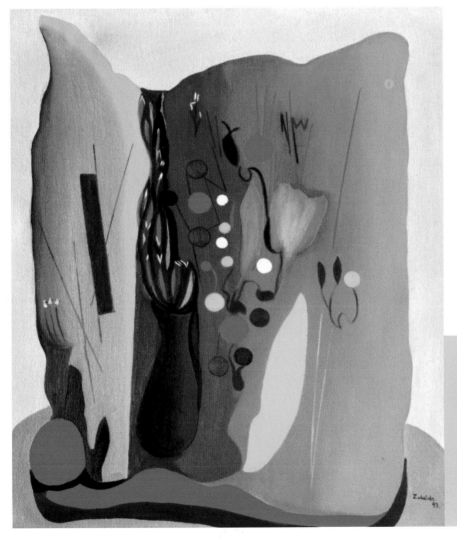

This painting, titled *Blue Vase*, is one of Zubeida Agha's creations. Agha completed *Blue Vase* in 1993, four years before he died.

Calligraphy and Handicrafts

The art of beautiful handwriting, which is called calligraphy, has been popular in Pakistan for hundreds of years. The calligraphy artists of Pakistan usually write out poems or verses from the Koran. Some also use calligraphy to make border patterns in books.

Every province in Pakistan has its own handicrafts. Punjab potters make clay toys that look like objects from the ancient Indus Valley civilization.

Some of the art that decorates Pakistan's mosques and other buildings are paintings that include calligraphy. Even objects such as plates and vases are often decorated with calligraphy.

These men are performing a traditional Sindhi folk dance. Many of Pakistan's folk dances are very lively.

Sindh province is also known for its pottery, as well as for embroidery and a craft known as mirrorwork, which is sewing tiny pieces of mirror onto cloth.

Folk Dancing

With so many ethnic groups, Pakistan has many different folk dances. In the Punjabi dance *bangra* (BAHNG-rah), men sing and dance in a circle around a drummer. The dance starts slowly, then gets faster and faster. *Khattak* (KHU-tuhk) is a Pashtun sword dance.

Leisure Time

Most of Pakistan's leisure activities are the kinds that bring friends and families together. After Friday prayers, Muslims often stay at the mosque to share news with friends. Hobbies and weekly trips to the market are some other activities that bring people together. Men in rural areas like to get together at *kushti* (wrestling) matches, and pigeon or camel races. Cities offer a greater variety of entertainment.

Pakistanis love to watch movies. Local movies are shown at cinemas, while films from Hollywood in the United States and Bollywood in India can be found for sale in many shops.

In Pakistan's cities, public parks are popular places for family activities, such as picnics and camel rides. Some cities also have amusement parks.

Children in Pakistan like to play board games. These boys are playing a game called ludo, which is a favorite board game in both India and Pakistan.

Television and Games

Most families in Pakistan have television sets. The programs they watch include news reports, quiz shows, soap operas, and reruns of old comedies from the West. Wealthier families with media players are able to watch new programs from the West that are recorded on disks or tapes and sold in shops.

Pakistani children play their own versions of games such as marbles, tag, and hide-and-seek, which are familiar to children all over the world. They also enjoy flying kites.

Cricket

The British introduced the game of cricket to British India in the 1700s. Today, Pakistanis play cricket locally, nationally, and internationally, and some of the world's best players, such as Imran Khan, Wasim Akram, and Mushtaq Ahmed, are from Pakistan. Like baseball, cricket is played with a bat and a ball and two teams, each with eleven players, but the rules for cricket are different than the rules for baseball.

Field hockey is a very popular sport in Pakistan. The country's national team has won three Olympic gold medals and four Hockey World Cup championships.

At the age of seventeen, Jahangir Khan (**left**) became the youngest winner of the World Open Championship in squash. Throughout the 1980s, Khan was a top player, winning the British Open Championship ten times in a row. He remains one of Pakistan's greatest athletes.

Other Sports

Field hockey, squash, and polo are just a few of the other sports played in Pakistan. Field hockey is the national sport of Pakistan. It is similar to ice hockey, but it is played on a field, hitting a small, hard ball, instead of on ice, which uses a puck. Squash is a two-player sport similar to racquetball. Polo is a team sport that is played on horseback. Players try to score points by hitting a ball with a stick, called a mallet, into the other team's goal.

Muslim Holy Days

For one month each year, all healthy, adult Muslims do not eat or drink during daylight hours. This time of fasting celebrates Ramadan, which is the holiest month in the Muslim calendar. Eid al-Fitr (EED AHL-fitr) is a festival that marks the end of Ramadan. **Bakr-Id** (BUK-rah EED), or Feast of the **Sacrifice**, is celebrated at the end of the Islamic year.

Muslims celebrate the end of Ramadan with prayers and feasts. These Muslims are praying at a mosque in Peshawar.

Islamabad celebrates Pakistan Day, on March 23, with a parade and fireworks. This holiday honors the 1940 resolution by which Muslims demanded an independent state.

Other Holidays

Besides religious holy days, Pakistan also has national holidays. August 14 is Independence Day. On this day, homes and businesses display the flag to celebrate India's break with Britain, which made Pakistan a separate nation. On September 6, Defense of Pakistan Day, military parades held throughout the country remember the **conflict**, which occurred in 1965 between Pakistan and India.

Food

Bread, rice, and vegetables are the most common foods eaten at daily meals in Pakistan. When they can afford to buy it, Pakistanis eat meat and poultry, too.

The kind of bread Pakistanis eat most often is called *chapati*. It is round and flat, like a tortilla, but when it is heated, chapati becomes soft and puffy. Chapati fried in butter is a popular bread called *paratha* (puh-RAH-tah).

Pakistani cooking uses a lot of herbs and spices, including red and green chilies, garlic, and ginger. Yogurt is an ingredient in many recipes because it helps make the taste of hot spices milder.

Each province in Pakistan has its own special dishes. Punjab province is known for its bread and different kinds of spiced legumes, known as dal, while Sindh province specializes in seafood dishes.

Besides eating plain white rice, many Pakistanis enjoy *biryani* (bir-YAH-nee), which is rice that has been cooked in a meat sauce.

Favorite vegetable dishes include dal, which is lentils, beans, or peas spiced with garlic, onions, chilies, cloves, ginger, and black pepper.

Tea, usually with milk and lots of sugar added, is Pakistan's most popular drink. *Lassi* (LASS-ee), a combination of yogurt and mango juice, is another favorite Pakistani beverage.

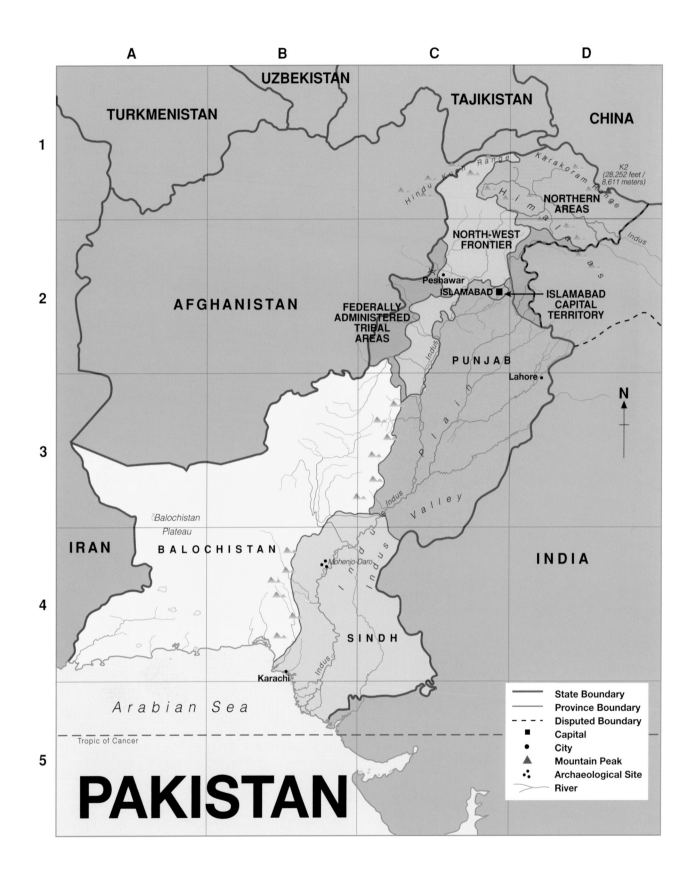

This man is making sweets to sell at a market in Peshawar.

Afghanistan A3–D1
Arabian Sea A4–C5

Balochistan (province)
   A4–C3
Balochistan Plateau
   A3–A4

China D1

Federally Administered
   Tribal Areas C2

Himalayas C1–D2
Hindu Kush
   Range C1

India C5–D2
Indus Plain B4–C3
Indus River B5–D2
Indus Valley C3–C4
Iran A1–A4
Islamabad C2
Islamabad Capital
   Territory C2

K2 D1
Karachi B4
Karakoram
   Range D1

Lahore D3

Mohenjo-Daro B4

Northern Areas C1–D2
North-West Frontier
   (province) C1–C3

Peshawar C2
Punjab (province)
   C3–D2

Sindh (province)
   B3–C5

Tajikistan B1–D1
Turkmenistan A1–B1

Uzbekistan B1

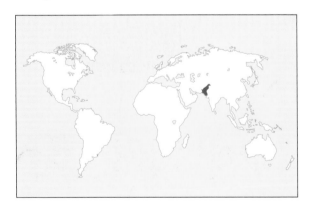

Quick Facts

Official Name Islamic Republic of Pakistan

Capital Islamabad

Official Languages Urdu, English

Population 176,242,949

Land Area 310,402 square miles (803,940 square kilometers)

Administrative Balochistan, Federally Administered Tribal Areas, Islamabad Capital Territory, North-West Frontier, Punjab, Sindh

Highest Point K2 (28,252 feet/8,611 meters)

Main River Indus

Main Religion Islam

National Holidays Pakistan Day (March 23), Independence Day (August 14), Defense of Pakistan Day (September 6), Birth and death anniversaries of Muhammad Ali Jinnah (December 25 and September 11)

Religious Festivals Ramadan, Bakr-Id, Eid al-Fitr

Currency Pakistan Rupee (85.02 PKR = U.S. $1 as of 2010)

This man is wearing a round, flat wool cap called a *hunza*. It is part of the traditional clothing worn by the Pashtun people, who live in North-West Frontier province.

Glossary

alpine: Related to area of land at very high elevations, especially a mountain slope above the timberline.

ancestor: Family member from past generations.

Aryans: People who settled in the regions of Iran and northern India around 1500 BCE.

Bakr-Id: A Muslim holy day or festival honoring the faith of Abraham, who, according to the Bible, was willing to sacrifice his only son to show his belief in God.

civilization: A highly developed society with an established government, culture, and a written history.

conflict: A fight, struggle, or clash due to opposing views or interests.

corruption: Dishonesty or illegal activity, usually to gain money or power.

coup: A sudden military action to take over a government.

crescent: A thin, curved moon shape.

diverse: Having many differences and much variety.

ethnic: Related to a group of people from a particular country or culture.

federal republic: A nation in which the citizens elect representatives to run the central government.

fertile: Able to support growth or produce offspring.

flourished: Grew or developed quickly and successfully.

humid: Damp, usually describing the amount of moisture in the air.

literacy: The ability to read and write.

mural: Large picture painted directly on walls or ceilings.

parliament: An official government body of elected representatives who make the laws of their country.

plateau: A wide area of high, flat land.

refuge: To look for safety and protection in another place.

sacrifice: The act of giving up personal needs or wants so that others will have what they need or want.

shantytown: Section of city where people live in crudely built shelters.

Sikh: Belonging to a religion of India known as Sikhism, which preaches the teachings of its founder, Guru Nanak, and the other nine holy Gurus who came after him.

For More Information

Books

Crompton, Samuel Willard. *Pakistan*. New York: Chelsea House Publications, 2007.

Donaldson, Madeline. *Pakistan*. Minneapolis, MN: Lerner Classroom, 2008.

Fazzi, Cindy. *How to Draw Pakistan's Sights and Symbols*. New York: PowerKids Press, 2005.

Lynch, Emma. *We're From Pakistan*. Chicago, IL: Heinemann Library, 2005.

Malik, Iftikhar H. *Culture and Customs of Pakistan*. Westport, CT: Greenwood Press, 2005.

Morgan, Sally. *Pakistan*. London: Hodder Wayland, 2007.

Razzak, Shazia. *P Is for Pakistan*. London: Frances Lincoln Children's Books, 2007.

DVDs

Globe Trekker Pakistan. (Pilot Productions, 2009).

Long Live Pakistan. (ARTE, 2008).

The Miseducation of Pakistan. (Choices, Inc, 2007).

Websites

www.enchantedlearning.com/asia/pakistan/flag/

Learn more about Pakistan's national flag. There are also pictures to print out for coloring.

www.harappa.com/har/har0.html

Discover more about the Indus civilization, whose people were among Pakistan's earliest inhabitants.

www.katw.org/pages/sitepage.cfm?id=114

Read the account of Miraal, a little girl who lives in Pakistan with her family.

library.thinkquest.org/CR0212302/pakistan.html

More on the Pakistani way of life, told from a child's perspective.

Index